Cheesecakes

baked and chilled

THE AUSTRALIAN
Women's Weekly

contents

I don't know anyone who doesn't like cheesecakes – they're so glamorous and decadent. Not for everyday certainly, but for a family get-together, a celebration, even a picnic or barbecue, a cheesecake is just the thing. They're wickedly rich, there's no getting around that, but they're so elegant, so creamy, so absolutely delicious. We're confident you'll love these recipes and make your favourites again and again.

Pamela Clark

Food Director

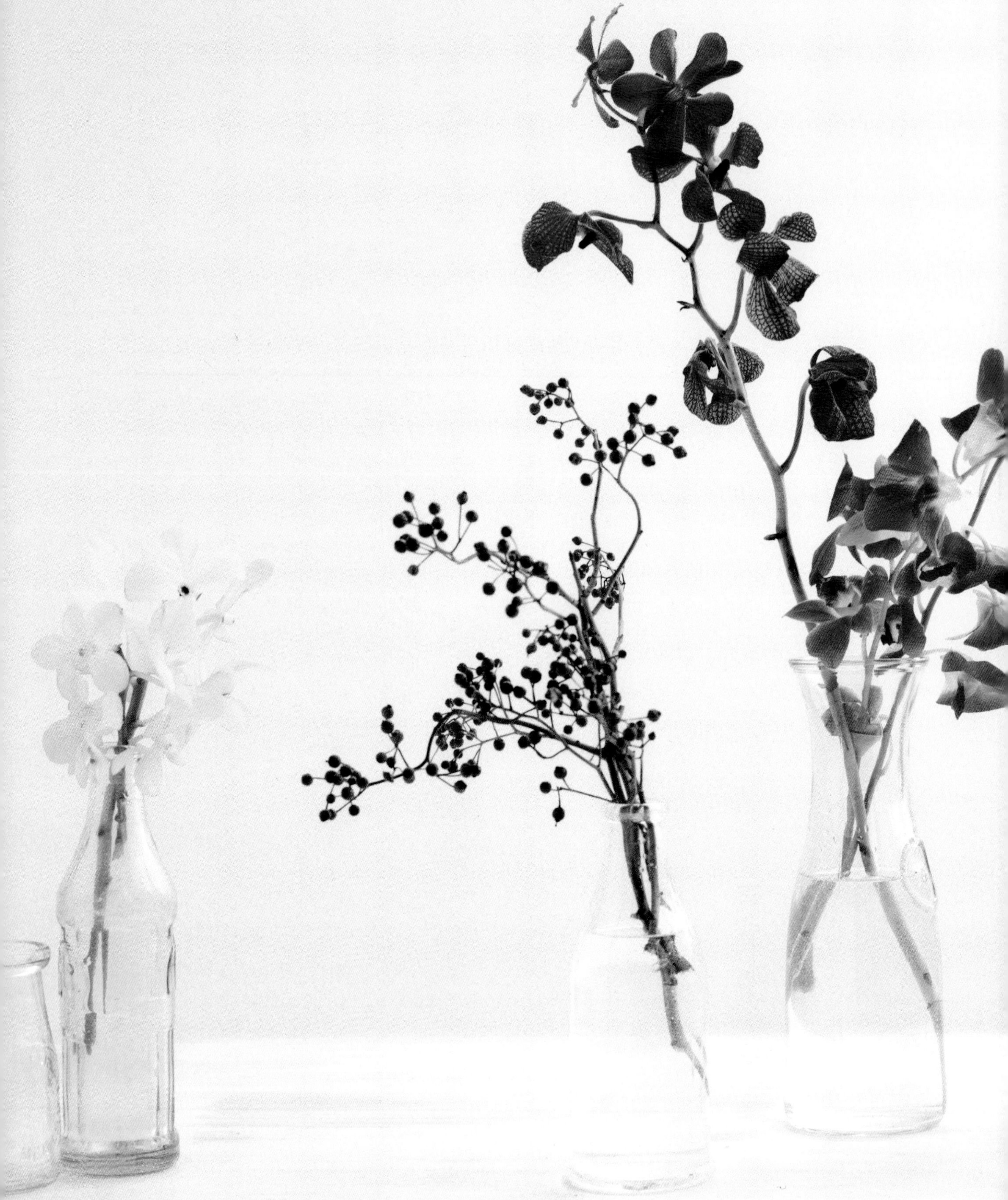

Here's a simple recipe for sweet success: whether you choose classic or less predictable flavours and ingredients, it's never a mistake to serve cheesecake. Everything that makes them delicious – their rich, creamy density, their sweet, saucy toppings, their unexpectedly delicious bases – are all bliss to the senses. And, as if that isn't enough, they can be made ahead. With their sophisticated tastes and simple preparation, these versatile recipes solve the never-ending dilemma of what to serve for dessert.

baked

Originating in lavish patisseries and coffee houses in Europe,
the timeless elegance of the simple baked cheesecake has
since been claimed by sweet-tooths the world over.

lemon curd

250g plain sweet biscuits
125g butter, melted

Filling
750g cream cheese, softened
2 teaspoons finely grated
   lemon rind
½ cup (110g) caster sugar
3 eggs

Lemon curd
45g butter
½ cup (110g) caster sugar
1 egg, beaten lightly, strained
1 teaspoon finely grated
   lemon rind
2 tablespoons lemon juice

1 Process biscuits until fine. Add butter, process until combined. Press mixture over base and side of 22cm springform tin. Place tin on oven tray; refrigerate 30 minutes.
2 Preheat oven to 160°C/140°C fan-forced.
3 Make filling by beating cheese, rind and sugar in medium bowl with electric mixer until smooth; beat in eggs, one at a time. Pour filling into tin; bake about 1 hour. Cool cheesecake in oven with door ajar.
4 Make lemon curd.
5 Spread cheesecake with lemon curd; refrigerate 3 hours or overnight.

Lemon curd
Combine ingredients in small heatproof bowl. Place bowl over small saucepan of simmering water (water must not touch bottom of bowl); cook, stirring constantly, about 20 minutes or until mixture coats the back of a spoon. Remove bowl from saucepan immediately; cover curd with plastic wrap, cool to room temperature.

Serves 10

lemon meringue

1½ cups (225g) plain flour
¼ cup (40g) icing sugar
125g cold butter, chopped
2 egg yolks
1 tablespoon iced water

Filling
375g cream cheese, softened
1 tablespoon finely grated
   lemon rind
1 egg
1 egg yolk
1 tablespoon lemon juice
1 tablespoon plain flour
½ cup (180g) lemon-flavoured
   spread

Meringue
2 egg whites
½ cup (110g) caster sugar
½ teaspoon cornflour

1 Grease six deep 10cm fluted loose-based flan tins.
2 Process flour, icing sugar and butter until crumbly. Add egg yolks and the water, pulse until ingredients come together. Knead pastry on floured surface until smooth. Wrap in plastic; refrigerate 30 minutes.
3 Divide pastry into six portions; roll each between sheets of baking paper until large enough to line prepared tins. Ease dough into tins, press into sides; trim edges. Refrigerate 30 minutes.
4 Preheat oven to 200°C/180°C fan-forced.
5 Cover pastry cases with baking paper, fill with dried beans or rice; place on oven tray. Bake 10 minutes. Remove paper and beans; bake about 10 minutes or until pastry is browned lightly. Cool.
6 Reduce oven temperature to 160°C/140°C fan-forced.

7 Make filling by beating cheese, rind, egg and egg yolk in small bowl with electric mixer until smooth. Beat in juice, flour and lemon spread.
8 Divide filling among pastry cases. Bake about 25 minutes; cool in oven with door ajar. Refrigerate 3 hours or overnight.
9 Preheat oven to 240°C/220°C fan-forced.
10 Make meringue.
11 Place cheesecakes on oven tray. Rough surface of cheesecakes with fork; pipe or spoon meringue over filling. Bake about 3 minutes or until browned lightly. Cool 10 minutes before serving.

Meringue
Beat egg whites in small bowl with electric mixer until soft peaks form; gradually add sugar, beating until sugar dissolves between additions. Fold in cornflour.

Makes 6

sour cream cheesecake

250g plain sweet biscuits
125g butter, melted
300g fresh blueberries

Filling
250g cottage cheese
250g cream cheese
2 teaspoons finely grated
   lemon rind
¾ cup (165g) caster sugar
3 eggs
1 cup (240g) sour cream
¼ cup (60ml) lemon juice

1 Process biscuits until fine. Add butter, process until combined. Press mixture over base and side of 22cm springform tin. Place tin on oven tray; refrigerate 30 minutes.
2 Preheat oven to 160°C/140°C fan-forced.
3 Make filling by sieving cottage cheese into medium bowl; add cream cheese, rind and sugar. Beat with electric mixer until smooth; beat in eggs, one at a time, then sour cream and juice.
4 Pour filling into tin; bake about 1¼ hours. Cool in oven with door ajar.
5 Refrigerate cheesecake 3 hours or overnight.
6 Top cheesecake with blueberries. Dust with sifted icing sugar, if desired.

Serves 12

vanilla spice

¾ cup (110g) plain flour
¼ teaspoon ground cinnamon
pinch ground nutmeg
⅓ cup (75g) caster sugar
80g butter, melted
½ teaspoon vanilla extract
⅓ cup (45g) roasted hazelnuts,
    chopped coarsely
¼ cup (80g) apricot jam,
    warmed, strained

Filling
1 vanilla bean
250g cream cheese, softened
500g ricotta cheese
2 tablespoons lemon juice
⅔ cup (150g) caster sugar
2 eggs

1 Grease 24cm springform tin.
2 Sift flour, spices and sugar
into medium bowl, stir in butter,
extract and nuts. Press mixture
over base of tin. Place tin on
oven tray; refrigerate 30 minutes.
3 Preheat oven to 180°C/160°C
fan-forced.
4 Bake base about 20 minutes or
until browned lightly. Spread with
jam. Reduce oven temperature
to 150°C/130°C fan-forced.
5 Make filling by splitting vanilla
bean in half lengthways; scrape
seeds into medium bowl. Add
cheeses, juice and half the sugar;
beat, with electric mixer until
combined. Beat remaining sugar
and eggs in small bowl with
electric mixer about 5 minutes or
until thick and creamy; fold into
cheese mixture.
6 Pour filling into tin; bake about
35 minutes. Cool cheesecake in
oven with door ajar.
7 Refrigerate cheesecake 3 hours
or overnight. Serve cheesecake
with cream, if desired.

Serves 12

butterscotch pecan

150g plain chocolate biscuits
50g butter, melted

Filling
500g cream cheese, softened
1 teaspoon vanilla extract
¾ cup (165g) caster sugar
2 eggs
1 tablespoon plain flour
½ cup (60g) roasted pecans,
  chopped finely

Butterscotch topping
⅓ cup (75g) firmly packed
  brown sugar
40g butter
1 tablespoon cream

1 Preheat oven to 160°C/140°C fan-forced.
2 Process biscuits until fine. Add butter, process until combined. Press mixture over base of 20cm springform tin. Place tin on oven tray; refrigerate 30 minutes.
3 Make filling by beating cheese, extract and sugar in medium bowl with electric mixer until smooth; beat in eggs. Stir in flour and nuts.
4 Pour filling into tin; bake about 45 minutes. Cool cheesecake in oven with door ajar.
5 Make butterscotch topping by heating ingredients in small saucepan until smooth.
6 Spread topping over cheesecake. Refrigerate 3 hours or overnight.

Serves 8

cherry ripe chocolate

125g plain chocolate biscuits
75g butter, melted

Filling
425g can seeded black cherries
   in syrup, drained
500g cream cheese, softened
⅓ cup (75g) caster sugar
2 eggs
200g dark eating chocolate,
   melted
3 x 55g Cherry Ripe bars,
   chopped coarsely

1 Grease 24cm springform tin.
2 Process biscuits until fine. Add butter, process until combined. Press mixture over base of tin. Place tin on oven tray; refrigerate 30 minutes.
3 Preheat oven to 180°C/160°C fan-forced.
4 Make filling by placing cherries on absorbent paper. Beat cheese and sugar in medium bowl with electric mixer until smooth; beat in eggs, one at a time. Gradually beat in cooled chocolate; stir in Cherry Ripe and cherries.
5 Spread filling into tin; bake about 50 minutes. Cool in oven with door ajar.
6 Refrigerate cheesecake 3 hours or overnight. Serve topped with dark chocolate curls, if desired.

Serves 12

italian ricotta

90g butter, softened
¼ cup (55g) caster sugar
1 egg
1¼ cups (185g) plain flour
¼ cup (35g) self-raising flour

Filling
1kg ricotta
1 tablespoon finely grated
  lemon rind
¼ cup (60ml) lemon juice
1 cup (220g) caster sugar
5 eggs
¼ cup (40g) sultanas
¼ cup (80g) finely chopped
  glacé fruit salad

1 Grease 28cm springform tin.
2 Beat butter, sugar and egg in small bowl with electric mixer until combined.
3 Stir in half the sifted flours; then work in remaining flour with hand. Knead pastry lightly on floured surface until smooth, wrap in plastic; refrigerate 30 minutes.
4 Press pastry over base of tin; prick with fork. Place on oven tray; refrigerate 30 minutes.
5 Preheat oven to 200°C/180°C fan-forced.
6 Cover pastry with baking paper, fill with beans or rice; bake 10 minutes. Remove paper and beans; bake 15 minutes or until browned lightly. Cool.
7 Reduce oven temperature to 160°C/140°C fan-forced.
8 Make filling by processing cheese, rind, juice, sugar and eggs until smooth; stir in fruit.
9 Pour filling into tin; bake about 50 minutes. Cool cheesecake in oven with door ajar.
10 Refrigerate cheesecake 3 hours or overnight.
11 Serve cheesecake dusted with sifted icing sugar, if desired.

Serves 16

double choc rum 'n' raisin

⅓ cup (80ml) dark rum
1 cup (160g) coarsely
   chopped raisins
150g butter, chopped
100g dark eating chocolate,
   chopped coarsely
1 cup (220g) caster sugar
⅔ cup (160ml) water
1 cup (150g) plain flour
2 tablespoons cocoa powder
2 egg yolks

Filling
500g cream cheese, softened
½ cup (110g) caster sugar
3 eggs
250g dark eating chocolate,
   melted

1 Combine rum and raisins in small bowl, cover; stand 3 hours or overnight.
2 Preheat oven to 180°C/160°C fan-forced. Grease 20cm x 30cm lamington pan; line base with baking paper, extending paper 5cm over long sides.
3 Combine butter, chocolate, sugar and the water in medium saucepan; stir over low heat until smooth. Remove from heat; stir in sifted flour and cocoa, then egg yolks.
4 Pour mixture into pan; bake about 15 minutes. Cool in pan.
5 Make filling by beating cheese and sugar in medium bowl with electric mixer until smooth; beat in eggs, one at a time. Stir in cooled chocolate, then raisin mixture.
6 Pour filling over base; bake about 45 minutes. Cool cheesecake in oven with door ajar.
7 Refrigerate 3 hours or overnight. Serve dusted with sifted cocoa, if desired.

Serves 18

new york cheesecake

250g plain sweet biscuits
125g butter, melted

Filling
750g cream cheese,
 softened
2 teaspoons finely grated
 orange rind
1 teaspoon finely grated
 lemon rind
1 cup (220g) caster sugar
3 eggs
¾ cup (180g) sour cream
¼ cup (60ml) lemon juice

Sour cream topping
1 cup (240g) sour cream
2 tablespoons caster sugar
2 teaspoons lemon juice

1 Process biscuits until fine. Add butter, process until combined. Press mixture over base and side of 24cm springform tin. Place tin on oven tray; refrigerate 30 minutes.
2 Preheat oven to 180°C/160°C fan-forced.
3 Make filling by beating cheese, rinds and sugar in medium bowl with electric mixer until smooth. Beat in eggs, one at a time, then cream and juice.
4 Pour filling into tin; bake 1¼ hours. Remove from oven; cool 15 minutes.
5 Make sour cream topping by combining ingredients in small bowl; spread over cheesecake.
6 Bake cheesecake 20 minutes; cool in oven with door ajar.
7 Refrigerate cheesecake 3 hours or overnight.

Serves 12

low-fat lemon and blackberry

200g low-fat cottage cheese
250g light spreadable
   cream cheese
2 teaspoons finely grated
   lemon rind
¾ cup (165g) caster sugar
2 eggs
⅓ cup (55g) semolina
¼ cup (35g) self-raising flour
¼ cup (60ml) buttermilk
200g fresh or frozen
   blackberries

1 Preheat oven to 160°C/140°C fan-forced. Grease 20cm springform tin; line base with baking paper. Place tin on oven tray.
2 Beat cheeses, rind and sugar in medium bowl with electric mixer until smooth; beat in eggs, one at a time. Stir in semolina and sifted flour, then buttermilk.
3 Pour mixture into tin, sprinkle with blackberries; bake about 1 hour. Cool cheesecake in oven with door ajar.
4 Refrigerate cheesecake 3 hours or overnight.
5 Serve dusted with sifted icing sugar, if desired.

Serves 12

sticky date

2 cups (280g) seeded dried dates
¾ cup (180ml) water
½ teaspoon bicarbonate of
   soda
750g cream cheese, softened
½ cup (110g) firmly packed
   brown sugar
¼ teaspoon ground cinnamon
¼ teaspoon mixed spice
2 eggs

Caramel sauce
25g butter
⅓ cup (75g) firmly packed
   brown sugar
⅓ cup (80ml) cream

1 Preheat oven to 160°C/140°C fan-forced. Grease 24cm springform tin; line base and side with baking paper. Place tin on oven tray.
2 Combine dates, the water and soda in small saucepan; bring to a boil, simmer 5 minutes. Cool mixture 5 minutes; blend or process until almost smooth.
3 Beat cheese and sugar in medium bowl with electric mixer until smooth. Add spices, eggs and date mixture; beat until combined.
4 Pour mixture into tin; bake about 1 hour. Cool cheesecake in oven with door ajar.
5 Refrigerate cheesecake 3 hours or overnight.
6 Make caramel sauce.
7 Serve cheesecake drizzled with warm or cold sauce.

Caramel sauce
Combine ingredients in small saucepan; stir over low heat, until smooth. Bring to a boil; remove from heat.

Serves 12

jaffa liqueur slice

250g plain chocolate biscuits
150g butter, melted

Filling
3 eggs
¾ cup (165g) caster sugar
500g cream cheese, softened
100g dark eating chocolate,
  melted
1 tablespoon finely grated
  orange rind
2 tablespoons Cointreau

Chocolate ganache
150g dark eating chocolate,
  chopped coarsely
¼ cup (60ml) cream

1 Grease 19cm x 29cm slice pan; line base with baking paper, extending paper 5cm over long sides.
2 Process biscuits until fine. Add butter; process until combined. Press mixture over base of pan; refrigerate 30 minutes.
3 Preheat oven to 160°C/140°C fan-forced.
4 Make filling by beating eggs and sugar in small bowl with electric mixer until thick and creamy. Beat cheese in medium bowl with electric mixer until smooth; beat in egg mixture in two batches.
5 Pour half the cheese mixture into another medium bowl. Stir cooled chocolate into one bowl, and rind and Cointreau into the other bowl. Pour both mixtures into pan, swirl with skewer; bake about 25 minutes. Cool cheesecake in oven with door ajar.
6 Make chocolate ganache.
7 Spread ganache over cheesecake; refrigerate 3 hours or overnight.

Chocolate ganache
Combine ingredients in small saucepan; stir over low heat until smooth. Cool 10 minutes.

Serves 12

mixed spice with honey syrup

250g plain sweet biscuits
125g butter, melted

Filling
500g cream cheese, softened
½ cup (110g) firmly packed
    brown sugar
2 teaspoons vanilla extract
1 teaspoon mixed spice
½ cup (125ml) cream
3 egg yolks
2 egg whites

Honey syrup
2 cinnamon sticks
4 strips lemon rind
⅓ cup (120g) honey
1 tablespoon water
¾ teaspoon gelatine

1 Grease deep 19cm square cake pan; line base and sides with baking paper, extending paper 5cm above edges of pan.
2 Process biscuits until fine; add butter, process until combined. Press mixture over base of pan; refrigerate 30 minutes.
3 Preheat oven to 160°C/140°C fan-forced.
4 Make filling by beating cheese, sugar, extract and spice in medium bowl with electric mixer until smooth; beat in cream and egg yolks.
5 Beat egg whites in small bowl with electric mixer until soft peaks form; fold into cream cheese mixture.
6 Pour filling into pan; bake about 50 minutes. Cool cheesecake in oven with door ajar.
7 Refrigerate cheesecake 3 hours or overnight.
8 Make honey syrup.
9 Serve cheesecake with warm syrup.

Honey syrup
Combine ingredients in small saucepan, bring to a boil; remove from heat.

Serves 9

orange and roasted plum tart

1½ cups (225g) plain flour
¼ cup (40g) icing sugar
125g cold butter, chopped
2 egg yolks
1 tablespoon iced water
8 small plums (560g), quartered
2 tablespoons orange juice
2 tablespoons brown sugar

Filling
500g cream cheese, softened
1 tablespoon finely grated
  orange rind
⅔ cup (150g) caster sugar
2 eggs
½ cup (120g) sour cream
2 tablespoons plain flour
⅓ cup (80ml) orange juice

1 Grease 19cm x 27cm rectangular loose-based flan tin or 26cm springform tin.
2 Process flour, icing sugar and butter until crumbly. Add egg yolks and the water; pulse until ingredients come together. Knead pastry on floured surface until smooth. Wrap in plastic; refrigerate 30 minutes.
3 Roll pastry between sheets of baking paper until large enough to line tin; press into sides, trim edges. Refrigerate 30 minutes.
4 Preheat oven to 180°C/160°C fan-forced.
5 Cover pastry with baking paper, fill with dried beans or rice; place on oven tray. Bake 10 minutes. Remove paper and beans; bake 10 minutes or until pastry is browned lightly. Cool.

6 Reduce oven temperature to 160°C/140°C fan-forced.
7 Make filling.
8 Pour filling into tin; bake about 50 minutes. Cool tart; refrigerate 3 hours.
9 Increase oven temperature to 200°C/180°C fan-forced. Place plums in single layer on oven tray, sprinkle with juice and sugar. Roast plums about 20 minutes or until soft. Cool.
10 Serve tart topped with roasted plums.

Filling
Beat cheese, rind and sugar in medium bowl with electric mixer until smooth. Beat in eggs, one at a time. Add remaining ingredients; beat until smooth.

Serves 8

cinnamon and apple

1 sheet ready-rolled
  shortcrust pastry
2 medium golden delicious
  apples (300g), unpeeled,
  sliced thinly
1 tablespoon lemon juice
1 tablespoon demerara sugar

Filling
750g cream cheese, softened
¾ cup (165g) caster sugar
1 teaspoon ground cinnamon
3 eggs, separated
¾ cup (180ml) cream

1 Preheat oven to 180°C/160°C fan-forced. Grease 24cm springform tin; place on oven tray.
2 Cut pastry into 24cm round, place in tin; prick well with a fork. Bake about 20 minutes or until browned lightly. Cool 5 minutes.
3 Make filling by beating cheese, sugar, cinnamon and egg yolks in medium bowl with electric mixer until smooth; beat in cream. Beat egg whites in small bowl with electric mixer until soft peaks form; fold into cheese mixture in two batches. Pour filling into tin.
4 Combine apple slices and lemon juice in small bowl. Arrange slices, slightly overlapping, over filling; sprinkle with sugar.
5 Bake about 50 minutes. Cool in oven with door ajar.
6 Refrigerate cheesecake 3 hours or overnight.

Serves 12

celebration cheesecake

500g fruit cake, cut into
   1cm slices
1 medium pink grapefruit (425g),
   segmented
2 large oranges (600g),
   segmented
250g strawberries, halved
120g fresh raspberries
150g fresh blueberries

Filling
750g cream cheese, softened
300g sour cream
1 teaspoon vanilla extract
1 cup (220g) caster sugar
¼ cup (60ml) brandy
½ teaspoon ground nutmeg
3 eggs

Toffee
1 cup (220g) caster sugar
1 cup (250ml) water

1 Preheat oven to 180°C/160°C fan-forced. Grease 26cm springform tin; line base with baking paper.
2 Cover base of tin with cake slices; bake 10 minutes. Reduce oven temperature to 150°C/130°C fan-forced.
3 Make filling by beating cheese, sour cream, extract, sugar, brandy and nutmeg in large bowl with electric mixer until smooth. Beat in eggs, one at a time.
4 Pour filling into tin; bake about 45 minutes. Cool cheesecake in oven with door ajar.
5 Refrigerate cheesecake 3 hours or overnight.
6 Make toffee.
7 Remove cheesecake from tin, to serving plate; top with fruit. Drizzle toffee over fruit.

Toffee
Stir sugar and the water in medium heavy-based frying pan over high heat until sugar dissolves. Boil, without stirring, uncovered, 10 minutes or until mixture is golden brown in colour. Remove from heat; stand until bubbles subside before using.

Serves 16

white chocolate and cranberry

100g plain sweet biscuits
50g butter, melted
150g frozen cranberries

Filling
¼ cup (60ml) thickened cream
180g white eating chocolate,
    chopped coarsely
375g cream cheese, softened
1 teaspoon finely grated
    orange rind
½ cup (110g) caster sugar
1 egg

1 Preheat oven to 150°C/130°C fan-forced. Line 6-hole Texas (¾ cup/180ml) muffin pan with paper cases or freeform cases, made from 17cm square sheets of baking paper. (You can also use a 22cm springform tin.)
2 Process biscuits until fine. Add butter, process until combined. Divide mixture among paper cases; press firmly over base of pan. Refrigerate 30 minutes.
3 Make filling by combining cream and 130g of the chocolate in small saucepan; stir over low heat until smooth.
4 Beat cheese, rind, sugar and egg in small bowl with electric mixer until smooth. Stir in cooled chocolate mixture.
5 Divide mixture among cases, sprinkle with cranberries. Bake about 30 minutes. Cool in oven with door ajar.
6 Refrigerate cheesecakes 3 hours.
7 Melt remaining chocolate; drizzle over cheesecakes.

Makes 6

triple coconut

90g coconut macaroons
125g plain sweet biscuits
125g butter, melted

Filling
250g cream cheese, softened
½ cup (110g) caster sugar
300g sour cream
2 tablespoons Malibu
2 x 140ml cans coconut milk
½ cup (40g) desiccated coconut,
    roasted
¼ cup (35g) cornflour
3 eggs

Glaze
100g dark eating chocolate,
    chopped coarsely
60g unsalted butter, chopped

1 Preheat oven to 160°C/140°C
fan-forced.
2 Process macaroons and biscuits
until fine. Add butter, process
until combined. Press mixture
over base and side of 26cm
springform tin. Place tin on oven
tray; refrigerate 30 minutes.
3 Make filling by beating cheese,
sugar, sour cream, Malibu,
coconut milk, coconut and
cornflour in medium bowl with
electric mixer until smooth. Beat
in eggs, one at a time.
4 Pour filling into tin; bake about
1 hour. Cool cheesecake in oven
with door ajar.
5 Refrigerate cheesecake 3 hours
or overnight.
6 Make glaze.
7 Spread glaze over cheesecake;
stand 20 minutes before serving.

Glaze
Combine ingredients in small
saucepan; stir over low heat
until smooth. Refrigerate until
mixture is spreadable.

Serves 12

cheesecake brownies

125g butter, chopped
150g dark eating chocolate,
  chopped coarsely
1 egg
⅔ cup (150g) caster sugar
¾ cup (110g) plain flour
¼ cup (35g) self-raising flour

Topping
250g cream cheese, softened
1 teaspoon vanilla extract
⅓ cup (75g) caster sugar
1 egg
½ cup (125ml) cream

1 Preheat oven to 180°C/160°C fan-forced. Grease deep 19cm-square cake pan; line base and sides with baking paper, extending paper 5cm over edge of sides.
2 Combine butter and chocolate in small saucepan; stir over low heat until smooth. Cool.
3 Beat egg and sugar in small bowl with electric mixer until thick and creamy. Stir in chocolate mixture and sifted flours.
4 Spread mixture into pan; bake 10 minutes.
5 Make topping.
6 Pour topping over brownie base; bake about 15 minutes. Cool in oven with door ajar.
7 Refrigerate brownies 3 hours.
8 Serve topped with fresh raspberries, if desired.

Topping
Beat cheese, extract, sugar and egg in small bowl with electric mixer until smooth; beat in cream.

Serves 12

spiced fig and orange

½ cup (80g) brazil nuts
125g plain sweet biscuits
80g butter, melted
1 cup (250ml) orange juice
1¼ cups (250g) finely chopped
   dried figs
1 cinnamon stick
pinch ground clove

Filling
250g cream cheese, softened
1 tablespoon finely grated
   orange rind
¾ cup (165g) caster sugar
1 cup (250g) mascarpone
2 eggs, separated

1 Grease 22cm springform tin.
2 Process nuts and biscuits until fine. Add butter; process until combined. Press mixture over base of tin. Place tin on oven tray; refrigerate 30 minutes.
3 Preheat oven to 160°C/140°C fan-forced.
4 Combine juice, figs, cinnamon and cloves in small saucepan; simmer, uncovered, 10 minutes or until most of the juice has been absorbed. Discard cinnamon stick. Spread fig mixture over crumb base in tin.
5 Make filling by beating cheese, rind and sugar in medium bowl with electric mixer until smooth. Add mascarpone and yolks; beat only until combined. Beat egg whites in small bowl with electric mixer until soft peaks form; fold into cheese mixture.
6 Pour filling over fig mixture; bake about 1¼ hours. Cool in oven with door ajar.
7 Refrigerate cheesecake 3 hours or overnight. Serve dusted with sifted icing sugar, if desired.

Serves 12

bistro cheesecake

250g plain sweet biscuits
125g butter, melted
½ teaspoon mixed spice

Filling
4 eggs
¾ cup (165g) caster sugar
500g cream cheese
1 tablespoon finely grated
    lemon rind

1 Process biscuits until fine. Add butter, process until combined. Press mixture over base and sides of 20cm springform tin. Place tin on oven tray; refrigerate 30 minutes.
2 Preheat oven to 160°C/140°C fan-forced.
3 Make filling by beating eggs and sugar in small bowl with electric mixer until thick and creamy. Beat cheese and rind in medium bowl with electric mixer until smooth. Add egg mixture to cheese mixture; beat until combined.
4 Pour filling into tin; bake about 50 minutes. Cool in oven with door ajar. Refrigerate 3 hours or overnight.
5 Serve cheesecake sprinkled with mixed spice.

Serves 10

black forest slice

425g can seedless black
  cherries in syrup
200g dark eating chocolate,
  melted
125g cream cheese, softened
125g mascarpone
½ cup (110g) caster sugar
⅔ cup (160ml) cream
1 egg, separated

Cherry topping
85g packet cherry flavoured
  jelly crystals
⅔ cup (160ml) boiling water

1 Preheat oven to 160°C/140°C fan-forced. Grease base of 19cm x 29cm slice pan; line base with baking paper, extending paper 5cm over long sides.
2 Drain cherries; reserve syrup. Make cherry topping.
3 Spread chocolate over base of pan; refrigerate until set.
4 Beat cheese, mascarpone, sugar, cream and egg yolk in small bowl with electric mixer until smooth; stir in cherries.
5 Beat egg white in small bowl with electric mixer until soft peaks form; fold into cream cheese mixture. Pour over chocolate base.
6 Bake about 35 minutes; cool in oven with door ajar.
7 Pour topping over cheesecake. Refrigerate overnight.

Cherry topping
Combine jelly crystals and the water in small bowl, stir until jelly is dissolved. Stir in ⅔ cup reserved cherry syrup; cool. Refrigerate jelly until thickened to the stage where it resembles unbeaten eggwhites.

Serves 8

rhubarb and almond jalousie

2 sheets ready-rolled puff pastry
1 tablespoon almond meal
1 egg white
1 tablespoon demerara sugar

Filling
250g cream cheese, softened
2 tablespoons caster sugar
2 tablespoons plain flour
1 egg

Topping
6 large stems (375g) trimmed
   rhubarb, cut into three
   crossways
¼ cup (55g) demerara sugar
2 tablespoons Grand Marnier

1 Preheat oven to 200°C/180°C fan-forced.
2 Make topping.
3 Cut one pastry sheet into 14cm x 24cm rectangle; cut remaining sheet into 18cm x 24cm rectangle. Leaving 2cm border around all sides, make about seven slits across width of larger sheet. Place smaller sheet on greased oven tray; sprinkle with almond meal.
4 Make filling by beating cheese and sugar in small bowl with electric mixer until smooth. Beat in flour and egg. Spread filling over pastry on tray leaving 2cm border around edges; spread with topping. Brush around border with egg white, place remaining pastry over filling; press edges together to seal.
5 Brush pastry with egg white; sprinkle with sugar. Bake about 30 minutes or until jalousie is browned lightly. Stand 1 hour before serving.

Topping
Combine ingredients in large frying pan; cook, stirring gently, until rhubarb softens. Cool.

Serves 8

vanilla with poached quince

125g granita biscuits
80g butter, melted

Filling
1 vanilla bean
500g cream cheese, softened
1½ cups (330g) caster sugar
2 eggs
½ cup (120g) sour cream
¼ cup (60ml) lemon juice

Poached quince
1 cup (220g) caster sugar
2 cups (500ml) water
2 medium quinces (700g),
   peeled, cored, quartered
2 strips lemon rind

1 Process biscuits until fine. Add butter; process until combined. Press mixture over base of 24cm springform tin. Place tin on oven tray; refrigerate 30 minutes.
2 Preheat oven to 160°C/140°C fan-forced.
3 Make filling by splitting vanilla bean in half lengthways, then scrape seeds into medium bowl; reserve pod for poached quinces. Add cheese, sugar, eggs, sour cream and juice to bowl; beat with electric mixer until smooth.
4 Pour filling into tin; bake about 35 minutes. Cool cheesecake in oven with door ajar. Refrigerate 3 hours or overnight.
5 Make poached quince.
6 Top cheesecake with quince; brush with quince syrup.

Poached quince
Stir sugar and the water in medium saucepan over heat until sugar dissolves. Add quince, rind and reserved vanilla pod; simmer, covered, about 2 hours or until quince is tender and rosy in colour. Cool quince in syrup. Remove quince from syrup; slice thinly. Simmer syrup, uncovered, until reduced by about half; cool.

Serves 12

glacé ginger and pineapple

150g butternut snap biscuits
75g butter, melted
¼ cup (60g) finely chopped
   glacé ginger
½ cup (115g) finely chopped
   glacé pineapple

Filling
500g cream cheese, softened
½ cup (110g) caster sugar
½ cup (120g) sour cream
2 tablespoons plain flour
3 eggs

1 Grease 24cm springform tin; line base and side with baking paper.
2 Process biscuits until fine. Add butter, process until combined. Press mixture over base of tin. Place tin on oven tray; refrigerate 30 minutes.
3 Preheat oven to 160°C/140°C fan-forced.
4 Make filling by beating cheese, sugar, cream and flour in medium bowl with electric mixer until smooth; beat in eggs, one at a time.
5 Combine ginger and pineapple; sprinkle one-third over base. Pour filling over fruit; bake 15 minutes. Sprinkle with remaining fruit; bake about 35 minutes. Cool in oven with door ajar.
6 Refrigerate cheesecake 3 hours or overnight.

Serves 12

chilled

Non-baked cheesecakes surprise with each bite – they're light and mousse-like, yet rich and creamy. Suitably special for a summer dinner party and delicious enough to eat all year round.

pineapple and coconut

180g coconut macaroons
60g butter, melted

Filling
1½ teaspoons gelatine
2 tablespoons water
250g cream cheese, softened
¼ cup (55g) caster sugar
1 cup (250ml) cream
¼ cup (60ml) Malibu

Pineapple topping
1 cup (250ml) pineapple juice
¼ small pineapple (225g),
   halved lengthways,
   sliced thinly

1 Grease 12-hole (¼ cup/60ml) mini cheesecake pan with removable bases.
2 Process macaroons until fine. Add butter; process until combined. Press a heaped tablespoon of mixture over base of each hole in pan. Refrigerate 30 minutes.
3 Make filling by sprinkling gelatine over the water in small heatproof jug; stand jug in small saucepan of simmering water. Stir until gelatine dissolves; cool 5 minutes.
4 Beat cheese and sugar in small bowl with electric mixer until smooth; beat in cream. Stir in Malibu and gelatine mixture. Divide mixture over bases; refrigerate overnight.
5 Make pineapple topping.
6 Serve cheesecakes topped with pineapple and juice.

Pineapple topping
Combine juice and pineapple in medium frying pan; simmer, about 10 minutes or until pineapple is soft. Remove pineapple from juice; simmer juice about 5 minutes or until thickened slightly. Cool.

Makes 12

berry bombe

450g madeira cake
2 teaspoons gelatine
2 tablespoons water
375g cream cheese, softened
½ cup (110g) caster sugar
300ml cream
1 cup (130g) frozen blackberries
1 tablespoon lemon juice

Meringue
4 egg whites
¾ cup (165g) caster sugar
1 teaspoon cornflour

1 Line 5-cup capacity pudding basin or bowl with plastic wrap, extending plastic 5cm over edge of basin.
2 Trim brown edges from cake. Cut two 1cm slices, lengthways, from cake; reserve remaining cake. Place cake slices together; cut out a 15cm round to fit the top of basin. Crumble remaining cake into basin; press crumbs firmly over base and side of basin.
3 Sprinkle gelatine over the water in small heatproof jug; stand jug in small saucepan of simmering water. Stir until gelatine dissolves. Cool 5 minutes.
4 Beat cheese and sugar in small bowl with electric mixer until smooth; beat in cream. Stir in gelatine mixture, then blackberries and juice. Pour mixture into basin; top with cake round. Cover with plastic wrap; refrigerate overnight.

5 Preheat oven to 240°C/220°C fan-forced.
6 Make meringue.
7 Turn cheesecake onto oven tray; discard plastic wrap. Spread meringue over bombe to enclose completely. Bake 3 minutes or until browned lightly. Serve immediately.

Meringue
Beat egg whites in small bowl with electric mixer until soft peaks form; gradually add sugar, beating between additions until sugar dissolves. Fold in cornflour.

Serves 8

63

sticky rhubarb on citrus

250g plain sweet biscuits
125g butter, melted
¼ teaspoon ground nutmeg

Filling
4 eggs, separated
1 cup (220g) caster sugar
2 tablespoons finely grated
   lemon rind
½ cup (125ml) lemon juice
½ cup (125ml) orange juice
1½ tablespoons gelatine
½ cup (125ml) water
500g cream cheese, softened
300ml thickened cream,
   whipped

Sticky rhubarb
8 large stems (500g) trimmed
   rhubarb, cut into 5cm lengths
¾ cup (165g) caster sugar
2 teaspoons lemon juice

1 Start making sticky rhubarb
by standing rhubarb and sugar
mixture overnight.
2 Grease eight 10cm round
springform tins or 28cm
springform tin; place on tray.
3 Process or blend biscuits until
fine. Add butter and nutmeg;
process until combined. Press
mixture over base of tins.
Refrigerate 30 minutes.
4 Make filling by combining
egg yolks, sugar, rind and juices
in medium heatproof bowl;
whisk over medium saucepan
of simmering water about
10 minutes or until thick and
foamy. Remove from heat.
5 Sprinkle gelatine over the
water in small heatproof jug;
stand jug in small saucepan
of simmering water. Stir until
gelatine dissolves; stir into
egg yolk mixture. Cool.
6 Beat cheese in large bowl with
electric mixer until smooth; beat in
egg yolk mixture in four batches.

7 Beat egg whites in small bowl,
with electric mixer until soft peaks
form. Fold whipped cream into
cheese mixture, then fold in
egg whites in two batches.
Divide mixture among tins.
Refrigerate overnight.
8 Remove rhubarb mixture from
refrigerator; continue making
sticky rhubarb.
9 Serve cheesecakes topped
with sticky rhubarb.

Sticky rhubarb
Combine rhubarb and sugar
in colander, stand colander in
a bowl; refrigerate overnight.
Combine rhubarb and drained
liquid in large frying pan; simmer,
uncovered about 5 minutes or
until rhubarb has softened. Fold
in juice; cool.

Makes 8

low-fat strawberries and cream

12 savoiardi sponge
   finger biscuits
½ cup (155g) strawberry jam,
   warmed
2 tablespoons hot water
350g strawberries
¼ cup (80g) strawberry jam,
   warmed, strained, extra
1 tablespoon lemon juice

Filling
1 tablespoon gelatine
¼ cup (60ml) water
500g low-fat ricotta
1 teaspoon finely grated
   lemon rind
¼ cup (55g) caster sugar
300ml low-fat cream
2 teaspoons lemon juice
3 egg whites

1 Grease base of deep 19cm square cake pan; line base and sides with plastic wrap, extending wrap 5cm over sides of pan. Trim one round edge from each biscuit. Place biscuits in single layer over base of pan; brush with combined jam and the hot water.
2 Make filling by sprinkling gelatine over the water in small heatproof jug; stand jug in small saucepan of simmering water. Stir until gelatine dissolves; cool 5 minutes.
3 Beat ricotta, rind and sugar in medium bowl with electric mixer until smooth; beat in cream and juice. Stir in gelatine mixture.
4 Beat egg whites in small bowl with electric mixer until soft peaks form; fold into ricotta mixture in 2 batches.
5 Pour filling over base. Refrigerate overnight.
6 Serve cheesecake topped with strawberries, brushed with combined extra jam and juice.

Serves 9

almond praline

100g butter, softened
2 tablespoons caster sugar
2 tablespoons rice flour
½ cup (75g) plain flour

Filling
2 teaspoons gelatine
2 tablespoons water
375g cream cheese, softened
½ cup (110g) caster sugar
300ml cream
1 teaspoon vanilla extract

Almond praline
½ cup (110g) caster sugar
¼ cup (60ml) water
¼ cup (35g) slivered almonds,
   roasted

1 Preheat oven to 150°C/130°C fan-forced. Grease 22cm springform tin.
2 Beat butter and sugar in small bowl with electric mixer until light and fluffy. Stir in sifted flours in two batches; knead on lightly floured surface until smooth.
3 Press mixture evenly over base of tin; bake shortbread about 35 minutes or until browned lightly. Cool in tin.
4 Make almond praline.
5 Remove base and shortbread from tin. Line tin with plastic wrap (see page 115). Replace base and shortbread; secure tin. Pull plastic wrap firmly up side of tin.
6 Make filling by sprinkling gelatine over the water in small heatproof jug; stand jug in small saucepan of simmering water. Stir until gelatine dissolves. Cool 5 minutes.
7 Beat cheese and sugar in medium bowl with electric mixer until smooth; beat in cream and extract. Stir in gelatine mixture. Finely chop praline; stir half into cheese mixture. Pour into tin; refrigerate overnight.
8 Serve cheesecake topped with remaining praline.

Almond praline
Combine sugar and the water in small saucepan; stir over low heat until sugar dissolves. Boil about 10 minutes or until mixture turns golden brown. Remove from heat. Place nuts in single layer on greased oven tray. Pour toffee over almonds. Stand at room temperature 10 minutes or until set.

Serves 10

date roll

2 tablespoons white sugar
1 cup (140g) seeded
   dried dates
¾ cup (180ml) boiling water
1 teaspoon bicarbonate of soda
50g butter, chopped
⅔ cup (165g) firmly packed
   brown sugar
2 eggs
¾ cup (110g) self-raising flour

Filling
1 teaspoon gelatine
1 tablespoon water
250g cream cheese, softened
½ cup (125ml) cream
2 tablespoons caster sugar

Butterscotch filling
½ cup (110g) firmly packed
   brown sugar
⅓ cup (80ml) cream
50g butter, chopped

1 Make butterscotch filling.
2 Preheat oven to 180°C/160°C
fan-forced. Grease 25cm x 30cm
swiss roll pan; line base with
baking paper, extending paper
5cm over long sides. Place a
piece of baking paper cut the
same size as swiss roll pan on
bench; sprinkle evenly with
white sugar.
3 Combine dates, the water and
soda in bowl of food processor,
cover with lid; stand 5 minutes.
Add butter and brown sugar;
process until almost smooth.
Add eggs and flour; pulse
until combined.
4 Pour mixture into pan; bake
about 15 minutes. Turn cake
onto sugared paper, peel baking
paper away; cut away crisp edges
from all sides of cake.
5 Gently roll cake loosely, with
the paper, from a long side; hold
for 30 seconds, then unroll. Cover
flat cake with tea towel; cool.
6 Make filling by sprinkling
gelatine over the water in small
heatproof jug; stand jug in small
saucepan of simmering water.
Stir until gelatine dissolves. Cool
5 minutes.

7 Beat cheese, cream and
sugar in small bowl with
electric mixer until smooth.
Stir in gelatine mixture.
8 Spread cake with filling;
dollop with butterscotch filling.
Roll cake, by lifting paper and
using it as a guide to roll.
9 Wrap roll in baking paper, then
foil; place on tray. Refrigerate
overnight before cutting.

Butterscotch filling
Combine ingredients in small
saucepan, stir over heat until
smooth; simmer, uncovered,
about 10 minutes or until
mixture thickens. Cool.

Serves 12

cookies and cream

You need an 80cm length of 50mm diameter PVC pipe, cut into 10cm lengths; ask the hardware store to do this for you, or use a hacksaw. This recipe will also fit into a 24cm springform tin. In this case, use a plain chocolate biscuit base (see page 19).

2 x 150g packets chocolate, cream-filled biscuits
50g dark eating chocolate, melted

Filling
2 teaspoons gelatine
2 tablespoons water
375g cream cheese, softened
1 teaspoon vanilla extract
½ cup (110g) caster sugar
300ml cream
180g white eating chocolate, melted

1 Stand eight cleaned 10cm lengths of PVC pipes on tray; grease each pipe and line with baking paper.
2 Place one biscuit in each pipe. Chop remaining biscuits into quarters.
3 Make filling by sprinkling gelatine over the water in small heatproof jug; stand jug in small saucepan of simmering water. Stir until gelatine dissolves; cool 5 minutes.
4 Beat cheese, extract and sugar in medium bowl with electric mixer until smooth; beat in cream. Stir in white chocolate, gelatine mixture and reserved biscuits.
5 Divide filling among pipes; refrigerate overnight.
6 Remove pipes and paper from cheesecakes; serve topped with chocolate.

Makes 8

roasted pear and almond tart

250g butternut snap biscuits
50g flaked almonds
125g butter, melted

Filling
2 teaspoons gelatine
2 tablespoons water
250g cream cheese, softened
⅓ cup (75g) caster sugar
¼ cup (90g) golden syrup
300ml thickened cream,
  whipped

Roasted pears
5 corella pears (500g), peeled,
  halved lengthways
⅓ cup (115g) golden syrup
30g butter

1 Grease 11cm x 34cm rectangular loose-based flan tin or 22cm springform tin.
2 Process biscuits and almonds until fine. Add butter; process until combined. Press mixture over base and side of tin. Refrigerate 30 minutes.
3 Make filling by sprinkling gelatine over the water in small heatproof jug; stand jug in small saucepan of simmering water. Stir until gelatine dissolves. Cool 5 minutes.
4 Beat cheese, sugar and golden syrup in small bowl with electric mixer until smooth. Stir in gelatine mixture; fold in cream. Pour filling into tin; refrigerate overnight.
5 Make roasted pears.
6 Serve cheesecake topped with pears and syrup.

Roasted pears
Preheat oven to 200°C/180°C fan-forced. Place pears in single layer, in large shallow baking dish; drizzle with golden syrup, dot with butter. Roast, uncovered, about 30 minutes, turning occasionally or until pears are soft. Cool to room temperature.

Serves 8

berry trifle

100g sponge cake,
   chopped coarsely
⅓ cup (80ml) Cointreau
300g frozen mixed berries

Filling
1 teaspoon gelatine
1 tablespoon water
250g cream cheese, softened
⅔ cup (150g) caster sugar
2 teaspoons lemon juice
300ml cream

Custard
¼ cup (30g) custard powder
¼ cup (55g) caster sugar
1½ cups (375ml) milk
20g butter
1 egg yolk

1 Divide sponge cake among eight 1⅓-cup (330ml) glasses; sprinkle with Cointreau and half of the berries.
2 Make filling by sprinkling gelatine over the water in small heatproof jug; stand jug in small saucepan of simmering water. Stir until gelatine dissolves; cool 5 minutes.
3 Beat cheese, sugar and juice in small bowl with electric mixer until smooth; beat in cream. Stir in gelatine mixture.
4 Divide mixture among glasses; top with remaining berries. Refrigerate 15 minutes.
5 Make custard.
6 Divide custard among glasses; refrigerate 30 minutes. Serve topped with fresh raspberries and blueberries, if desired.

Custard
Blend custard powder and sugar with ⅓ cup of the milk in small saucepan until smooth; stir in remaining milk. Stir over heat until mixture boils and thickens; remove from heat, stir in butter and egg yolk. Cover surface of custard with plastic wrap. Cool.

Serves 8

lemon ricotta

250g ginger nut biscuits
125g butter, melted

Filling
3 teaspoons gelatine
¼ cup (60ml) water
250g cream cheese
750g ricotta
1 tablespoon finely grated
   lemon rind
½ cup (110g) caster sugar
⅓ cup (80ml) lemon juice
300ml thickened cream,
   whipped

Passionfruit topping
½ cup (125ml) orange juice
2 tablespoons passionfruit pulp
1 tablespoon caster sugar
2 teaspoons gelatine

1 Process biscuits until fine.
Add butter, process until
combined. Press mixture over
base of 26cm springform tin.
Refrigerate 30 minutes.
2 Make filling by sprinkling
gelatine over the water in small
heatproof jug; stand jug in small
saucepan of simmering water.
Stir until gelatine dissolves;
cool 5 minutes.
3 Beat cheeses, rind, sugar
and juice in large bowl with
electric mixer until smooth.
Stir in gelatine mixture; fold in
cream. Spread filling into tin;
refrigerate overnight.
4 Make passionfruit topping.
5 Pour topping over cheesecake.
Refrigerate until set.

Passionfruit topping
Combine juice, passionfruit
and sugar in small saucepan;
stir over low heat until sugar is
dissolved. Remove from heat;
add gelatine, stir until dissolved.
Cool 15 minutes.

Serves 16

frozen peanut butter

250g chocolate chip biscuits
50g butter, melted
1 tablespoon milk

Filling
¾ cup (210g) crunchy
   peanut butter
½ cup (125ml) cream
250g cream cheese, softened
½ cup (110g) caster sugar

Hot chocolate sauce
200g dark eating chocolate,
   chopped coarsely
20g butter
½ cup (125ml) cream

1 Grease 24cm round loose-based flan tin.
2 Process biscuits until fine; add butter and milk, process until combined. Press mixture over base and side of tin. Freeze 30 minutes.
3 Make filling by combining peanut butter and cream in small saucepan; stir, over low heat until smooth. Cool.
4 Beat cheese and sugar in small bowl with electric mixer until smooth. Stir in peanut butter mixture.
5 Spread filling over crust; cover with foil, freeze 3 hours or overnight.
6 Make hot chocolate sauce; serve with cheesecake.

Hot chocolate sauce
Combine ingredients in small saucepan; stir over low heat until smooth.

Serves 16

mango macadamia meringue

½ cup (70g) roasted
   macadamia nuts
4 egg whites
¾ cup (165g) caster sugar

Filling
2 teaspoons gelatine
2 tablespoons water
250g cream cheese, softened
½ cup (110g) caster sugar
1 tablespoon lemon juice
300ml cream

Mango jelly
2 cups (500ml) mango puree
1 tablespoon gelatine

1 Preheat oven to 180°C/160°C fan-forced. Grease two 22cm springform tins; line bases and sides with baking paper.
2 Process half the nuts until fine. Chop remaining nuts coarsely.
3 Beat egg whites in small bowl with electric mixer until soft peaks form. Add sugar, 1 tablespoon at a time, beating until sugar dissolves between each addition. Fold in all nuts. Divide meringue between tins; bake 30 minutes. Cool meringues in oven with door ajar.
4 Make mango jelly.
5 Make filling by sprinkling gelatine over the water in small heatproof jug; stand jug in small saucepan of simmering water. Stir until gelatine dissolves; cool 5 minutes.
6 Beat cheese, sugar and juice in small bowl with electric mixer until smooth; beat in cream. Stir in gelatine mixture.

7 Remove paper collar from one of the meringue layers in tin. Line tin with plastic wrap (see page 115). Return meringue to tin, flatten with hand. Pour half the filling over meringue; refrigerate 15 minutes. Spread jelly over filling; cover, refrigerate 20 minutes. Spread remaining filling over jelly.
8 Remove remaining meringue and paper from tin. Place on top of cheesecake; press down gently. Refrigerate overnight.

Mango jelly
Place puree in small saucepan, sprinkle with gelatine; stir over low heat until gelatine is dissolved. Cool.

Serves 12

tiramisu

¼ cup (20g) medium ground
  espresso coffee
1 cup (250ml) boiling water
2 tablespoons caster sugar
⅓ cup (80ml) marsala
250g savoiardi sponge
  finger biscuits
150g chocolate-coated coffee
  beans, chopped coarsely

Filling
2 teaspoons gelatine
2 tablespoons water
125g cream cheese, softened
¼ cup (40g) icing sugar
250g mascarpone
2 tablespoons marsala
300ml thickened cream,
  whipped

1 Grease 24cm round
springform tin.
2 Combine coffee and the
water in coffee plunger; stand
4 minutes before plunging.
Combine coffee, sugar and
marsala in medium heatproof
bowl; cool 10 minutes.
3 Place ⅓ cup (80ml) coffee
mixture in small saucepan;
simmer, uncovered, until reduced
to about 1 tablespoon. Cool.
4 Cut each biscuit into 7cm
lengths; reserve end pieces. Dip
flat side of biscuit lengths one
at a time in remaining coffee
mixture; arrange biscuits, round
side out, around side of tin. Dip
reserved biscuit ends in coffee
mixture; place over base of tin.
5 Make filling by sprinkling
gelatine over the water in small
heatproof jug; stand jug in
small saucepan of simmering
water. Stir until gelatine
dissolves. Cool 5 minutes.

6 Beat cheese and sifted sugar
in medium bowl with electric
mixer until smooth. Add
mascarpone and marsala; beat
until combined. Stir in gelatine
mixture; fold in whipped cream.
7 Spread filling into tin. Drizzle
reduced coffee mixture over
cheesecake, pull skewer
backwards and forwards
several times for marbled
effect. Refrigerate overnight.
8 Serve cheesecake topped
with chocolate-coated
coffee beans.

Serves 12

mocha crème brûlée

75g butter, chopped
50g dark eating chocolate,
   chopped
½ cup (110g) caster sugar
¼ cup (60ml) water
1 tablespoon Kahlua
½ cup (75g) plain flour
1 tablespoon cocoa powder
1 egg yolk
1 tablespoon caster sugar, extra

Crème brûlée filling
2 teaspoons gelatine
2 tablespoons water
2 tablespoons Kahlua
2 teaspoons instant
   coffee granules
500g cream cheese, softened
½ cup (110g) caster sugar
2 teaspoons vanilla extract
1 cup (250ml) cream

1 Preheat oven to 160°C/140°C fan-forced. Grease 20cm x 30cm lamington pan; line base and sides with baking paper, extending paper 5cm over long sides.
2 Combine butter, chocolate, sugar, the water and liqueur in small saucepan. Stir over low heat until smooth.
3 Transfer mixture to small bowl; cool 10 minutes. Whisk in sifted flour and cocoa, then egg yolk. Pour mixture into pan; bake about 20 minutes. Cool in pan.
4 Cut six rounds from cake large enough to cover bases of six ¾ cup (180ml) heatproof dishes.
5 Make crème brûlée filling by sprinkling gelatine over the water and liqueur in small heatproof jug; stand jug in small saucepan of simmering water. Stir until gelatine dissolves; add coffee, stir until dissolved. Cool 5 minutes.

6 Beat cheese, sugar and extract in medium bowl with electric mixer until smooth; beat in cream. Add coffee mixture; beat until smooth. Divide filling among dishes; refrigerate 3 hours or overnight.
7 Preheat grill on highest setting. Sprinkle extra sugar evenly over cheesecakes. Using finger, press gently onto surface of cheesecakes; place under grill until tops have caramelised.

Serves 6

double chocolate mousse

125g plain chocolate biscuits
75g butter, melted
150g dark eating chocolate,
  melted

Filling
3 teaspoons gelatine
¼ cup (60ml) water
500g cream cheese, softened
½ cup (110g) caster sugar
2 eggs, separated
1 cup (250ml) cream
150g dark eating chocolate,
  melted
100g white eating chocolate,
  melted
2 tablespoons cream, extra

1 Line 22cm springform tin with plastic wrap (see page 115).
2 Process biscuits until fine. Add butter; process until combined. Press mixture over base of tin. Refrigerate 30 minutes.
3 Make filling by sprinkling gelatine over the water in small heatproof jug; stand jug in small saucepan of simmering water. Stir until gelatine dissolves; cool 5 minutes.
4 Beat cheese, sugar and egg yolks in medium bowl with electric mixer until smooth; beat in cream. Stir in dark chocolate and gelatine mixture.
5 Beat egg whites in small bowl with electric mixer until soft peaks form; fold into cheese mixture. Pour filling into tin.
6 Combine white chocolate and extra cream in small jug. Swirl white chocolate mixture through cheesecake mixture. Refrigerate overnight.
7 Spread dark chocolate over baking paper to a 20cm square. When set, break chocolate into small pieces.
8 Remove cheesecake from tin to serving plate. Press chocolate pieces around side of cheesecake.

Serves 12

triple chocolate cones

3 teaspoons gelatine
¼ cup (60ml) water
1 egg
500g cream cheese, softened
½ cup (110g) caster sugar
2 teaspoons vanilla extract
1¾ cups (430ml) cream
80g white eating chocolate,
  melted
80g milk eating chocolate
1 tablespoon Baileys Irish
  Cream
80g dark eating chocolate
1 tablespoon cocoa powder

1 Cut six 30cm squares from baking paper; fold squares in half diagonally. Place one triangle on bench with centre point towards you; curl one point towards you, turning it under where it meets the centre point. Hold these two points together with one hand then roll remaining point towards you to meet the other two, turning it under to form a cone. Staple or tape the cone securely to hold its shape; stand cone upright in a tall glass. Repeat with remaining triangles; place glasses on tray.
2 Sprinkle gelatine over the water in small heatproof jug; stand jug in small saucepan of simmering water. Stir until gelatine dissolves; cool 5 minutes.
3 Beat egg, cheese, sugar and extract in medium bowl with electric mixer until smooth; beat in cream. Stir in gelatine mixture.

4 Divide mixture into three bowls in 1-cup (250ml), 1½-cup (375ml) and 2-cup (500ml) quantities. Fold white chocolate into the 1-cup mixture; divide evenly among cones. Freeze 15 minutes or until layer is starting to set. Remove from freezer; scratch surface of cheesecake with fork.
5 Melt milk chocolate; fold into the 1½-cup mixture with Baileys. Divide evenly among cones. Freeze 15 minutes or until layer is just starting to set. Remove from freezer; scratch surface of cheesecake with fork.
6 Melt dark chocolate; fold into the 2-cup mixture with sifted cocoa. Divide evenly among cones. Cover cones loosely with plastic wrap; refrigerate overnight.
7 Place cones on serving plates; remove paper. Serve immediately, with fresh blueberries, if desired.

Serves 6

choc hazelnut éclairs

80g butter
1 cup (250ml) water
1 cup (150g) plain flour
4 eggs, beaten lightly
¼ cup (35g) roasted hazelnuts,
  chopped coarsely

Filling
⅔ cup (160ml) thickened cream
1½ tablespoons icing sugar
250g cream cheese, softened
2 tablespoons Frangelico
50g dark eating chocolate,
  chopped finely

Chocolate glaze
60g butter
125g dark eating chocolate,
  chopped coarsely

1 Preheat oven to 220°C/200°C fan-forced. Grease two oven trays.
2 Combine butter and the water in small saucepan; bring to a boil. Add flour; beat, over heat, with wooden spoon until mixture comes away from base and side of pan to form a smooth ball.
3 Transfer mixture to small bowl; gradually beat in egg with electric mixer until mixture becomes glossy.
4 Spoon choux pastry into piping bag fitted with 3cm plain tube. Pipe 6cm lengths of mixture, 3cm apart, onto trays; bake 10 minutes. Reduce oven temperature to 180°C/160°C fan-forced; bake about 10 minutes or until éclairs are browned lightly. Split éclairs in half, remove any soft centres; return to trays. Bake about 5 minutes or until éclairs are dried out. Cool.

5 Make filling by beating cream and sifted icing sugar in small bowl with electric mixer until soft peaks form. Beat cheese and Frangelico in small bowl with electric mixer until smooth. Fold in chocolate, then cream. Refrigerate.
6 Make chocolate glaze.
7 Spoon filling into 12 éclair halves. Dip remaining halves into chocolate glaze; sprinkle with nuts. When glaze is firm, sandwich éclair halves together.

Chocolate glaze
Combine butter and chocolate in small saucepan; stir over low heat until smooth.

Makes 12

mint chocolate truffle

You need an 80cm length of 50mm diameter PVC pipe, cut into 10cm lengths; ask the hardware store to do this for you, or use a hacksaw. This recipe will also fit into six 10cm round springform tins or a 24cm springform tin.

125g plain chocolate biscuits
35g Peppermint Crisp
    chocolate bar
75g butter, melted

Filling
2 teaspoons gelatine
2 tablespoons water
500g cream cheese, softened
½ cup (110g) caster sugar
¼ cup (60ml) crème de menthe
    liqueur
1½ cups (375ml) thickened
    cream, whipped

Truffles
2 tablespoons thickened cream
100g dark eating chocolate,
    chopped coarsely
2 x 35g Peppermint Crisp
    chocolate bars, chopped finely

1 Make truffles.
2 Stand eight 10cm lengths of cleaned PVC pipe on tray; line each pipe with baking paper.
3 Process biscuits and peppermint crisp until fine. Add butter; process until combined. Divide mixture among pipes; using end of wooden spoon, press mixture down evenly. Refrigerate 30 minutes.
4 Make filling by sprinkling gelatine over the water in small heatproof jug; stand jug in small saucepan of simmering water. Stir until gelatine dissolves. Cool 5 minutes.
5 Beat cream cheese and sugar in medium bowl with electric mixer until smooth. Stir in gelatine mixture and liqueur; fold in cream. Divide filling among pipes; refrigerate overnight.
6 Remove pipes and paper from cheesecakes. Serve topped with truffles and mint leaves, if desired.

Truffles
Combine cream and dark chocolate in small saucepan; stir over low heat until smooth. Transfer mixture to small bowl, cover; refrigerate 3 hours. Roll ½ teaspoonfuls of mixture into balls; place on tray. Roll balls in Peppermint Crisp; return to tray. Refrigerate truffles until firm.

Makes 8

rosewater and pistachio

125g butter, softened
1 cup (220g) caster sugar
2 eggs
1 cup (150g) roasted pistachios,
   chopped coarsely
2 cups (300g) self-raising flour
⅔ cup (160ml) milk
1 tablespoon icing sugar
¼ teaspoon ground cardamom

Filling
2 teaspoons gelatine
2 tablespoons water
125g cream cheese, softened
¾ cup (165g) caster sugar
2 tablespoons lemon juice
1 teaspoon rosewater
pink food colouring
1 cup (250g) mascarpone
300ml thickened cream,
   whipped

1 Preheat oven to 180°C/160°C fan-forced. Grease 22cm springform tin; line base with baking paper.
2 Beat butter and sugar in small bowl with electric mixer until light and fluffy. Beat in eggs, one at a time, until combined; transfer mixture to large bowl.
3 Stir in nuts, sifted flour and milk in two batches. Spread mixture in tin; bake about 50 minutes. Stand cake 5 minutes; turn onto wire rack to cool.
4 Make filling by sprinkling gelatine over the water in small heatproof jug; stand jug in small saucepan of simmering water. Stir until gelatine dissolves. Cool 5 minutes.
5 Beat cheese, sugar, juice and rosewater in medium bowl with electric mixer until smooth. Beat in enough colouring to tint mixture pale pink. Add mascarpone; beat until combined. Stir in gelatine mixture; fold in cream.
6 Split cake in half; return bottom layer to tin. Spread filling over cake; refrigerate 30 minutes. Top with remaining cake; refrigerate 3 hours.
7 Serve cheesecake dusted with sifted icing sugar and cardamom.

Serves 8

classic lemon

250g plain sweet biscuits
125g butter, melted

Filling
1 teaspoon gelatine
1 tablespoon water
250g cream cheese, softened
2 teaspoons finely grated
  lemon rind
395g can sweetened
  condensed milk
⅓ cup (80ml) lemon juice

Lemon rind syrup
⅓ cup (75g) caster sugar
⅓ cup (80ml) water
2 tablespoons shredded
  lemon rind

1 Process biscuits until fine. Add butter, process until combined. Press mixture over base and side of 20cm springform tin. Refrigerate 30 minutes.
2 Make filling by sprinkling gelatine over the water in small heatproof jug; stand jug in small saucepan of simmering water. Stir until gelatine dissolves; cool 5 minutes.
3 Beat cheese and rind in small bowl with electric mixer until smooth. Add condensed milk and juice; beat until smooth. Stir in gelatine mixture.
4 Pour filling into tin; refrigerate cheesecake overnight.
5 Make lemon rind syrup; serve with cheesecake.

Lemon rind syrup
Stir sugar and the water in small saucepan, over low heat, until sugar is dissolved; simmer 2 minutes. Add rind, simmer until syrup is thickened slightly; cool.

Serves 8

ginger cake with lime

250g butter, chopped
½ cup (110g) firmly packed
    dark brown sugar
⅔ cup (230g) golden syrup
12cm piece fresh ginger (60g),
    grated
¾ cup (180ml) cream
2 eggs
1 cup (150g) plain flour
1 cup (150g) self-raising flour
½ teaspoon bicarbonate of soda

Filling
½ teaspoon gelatine
1 tablespoon lime juice
125g cream cheese, softened
1 teaspoon finely grated
    lime rind
1 tablespoon caster sugar
¼ cup (60ml) cream

Lime syrup
½ cup (110g) caster sugar
½ cup (125ml) lime juice
½ cup (125ml) water
2 teaspoons finely grated
    lime rind

1 Preheat oven to 180°C/160°C fan-forced. Grease deep 22cm-round cake pan; line base and side with baking paper.
2 Combine butter, sugar, golden syrup and ginger in medium saucepan; stir over low heat until sugar dissolves. Remove from heat. Whisk in cream, then eggs and sifted flours and soda.
3 Pour mixture into pan; bake about 1 hour. Stand cake in pan 10 minutes; turn cake onto wire rack to cool.
4 Make filling by sprinkling gelatine over juice in small heatproof jug; stand jug in small saucepan of simmering water. Stir until gelatine dissolves. Cool 5 minutes. Beat cheese, rind, sugar and cream in small bowl with electric mixer until smooth. Stir in gelatine mixture.

5 Split cake horizontally a quarter of the way from the top; set aside. Place large piece of cake on serving plate. Using small teaspoon or melon baller, scoop 18 holes (at equal distances apart and not through to bottom) out of cake. Pour filling mixture into holes; replace top of cake. Cover; refrigerate overnight.
6 Make lime syrup.
7 Serve cake drizzled with lime syrup.

Lime syrup
Combine sugar, juice and the water in small saucepan; stir, over heat, until sugar dissolves. Boil, uncovered, 10 minutes or until syrup thickens slightly. Remove from heat; stir in rind. Cool.

Serves 12

palm sugar and lime

250g butternut snap biscuits
50g butter, melted

Filling
1 teaspoon gelatine
2 tablespoons lime juice
¼ cup (65g) grated palm sugar
250g cream cheese, softened
2 teaspoons finely grated
   lime rind
1 cup (250ml) cream

Palm sugar syrup
1 lime
½ cup (125ml) water
⅓ cup (90g) grated palm sugar

1 Grease 12-hole (¼ cup/60ml) mini cheesecake pan with removable bases.
2 Process biscuits until fine. Add butter; process until combined. Divide mixture among holes; press firmly. Refrigerate 30 minutes.
3 Make filling by sprinkling gelatine over juice in small heatproof jug; stand jug in small saucepan of simmering water. Stir until gelatine dissolves. Cool 5 minutes. Stir in sugar.
4 Beat cheese and rind in small bowl with electric mixer until smooth; beat in cream. Stir in gelatine mixture. Divide filling mixture among holes; refrigerate overnight.
5 Make palm sugar syrup.
6 Serve cheesecakes with palm sugar syrup.

Palm sugar syrup
Remove rind from lime; cut into thin strips. Stir the water and sugar in small saucepan over low heat until sugar dissolves. Boil, uncovered, without stirring, about 5 minutes or until syrup thickens slightly. Remove from heat; add rind. Cool.

Serves 12

maple pecan

185g ginger nut biscuits
60g butter, melted

Filling
3 teaspoons gelatine
¼ cup (60ml) water
500g cream cheese, softened
⅓ cup (55g) firmly packed
   brown sugar
300ml cream
½ cup (125ml) maple syrup

Topping
1¼ cups (175g) pecans,
   chopped coarsely
2 tablespoons maple syrup

1 Grease deep 19cm square cake pan; line base and sides with two sheets baking paper, extending paper 5cm above edges of pan.
2 Process biscuits until fine. Add butter; process until combined. Press mixture over base of pan; refrigerate 30 minutes.
3 Make filling by sprinkling gelatine over the water in small heatproof jug; stand jug in small saucepan of simmering water. Stir until gelatine dissolves. Cool 5 minutes.
4 Beat cheese and sugar in medium bowl with electric mixer until smooth; beat in cream and maple syrup. Stir in gelatine mixture.
5 Pour filling mixture into pan; refrigerate overnight.
6 Make topping.
7 Serve cheesecake sprinkled with topping.

Topping
Preheat oven to 240°C/220°C fan-forced. Combine nuts and maple syrup in small bowl; spread mixture onto greased oven tray. Roast 10 minutes or until browned lightly; cool.

Serves 12

malted milkshake

200g chocolate mudcake
90g Maltesers, crushed
⅓ cup (80ml) chocolate liqueur

Filling
3 teaspoons gelatine
¼ cup (60ml) water
500g cream cheese, softened
½ cup (110g) caster sugar
½ cup (60g) powdered malt
1 cup (250ml) thickened cream
2 eggs, separated
100g dark eating chocolate,
   melted

Topping
55g Maltesers

1 Cut mudcake into 1cm cubes;
divide among eight 1 cup (250ml)
glasses. Top with crushed
Maltesers and liqueur.
2 Make filling by sprinkling
gelatine over the water in small
heatproof jug; stand jug in small
saucepan of simmering water.
Stir until gelatine dissolves.
Cool 5 minutes.
3 Beat cheese, sugar and malt in
medium bowl with electric mixer
until smooth; beat in cream
and egg yolks. Stir in gelatine
mixture, then chocolate.
4 Beat egg whites in small
bowl with electric mixer until
firm peaks form; fold into
chocolate mixture.
5 Divide filling among glasses;
refrigerate overnight.
6 Serve cheesecake topped with
whole Maltesers.

Serves 8

berry nougat

125g butternut snap biscuits
60g butter, melted
100g almond nougat,
    chopped finely
300g frozen raspberries

Filling
2 teaspoons gelatine
2 tablespoons water
375g cream cheese, softened
¼ cup (55g) caster sugar
2 teaspoons lemon juice
300ml cream

1 Line 22cm springform tin with plastic wrap (see page 115).
2 Process biscuits until fine. Add butter; process until combined. Stir in nougat. Press mixture over base of tin. Refrigerate 30 minutes.
3 Make filling by sprinkling gelatine over the water in small heatproof jug; stand jug in small saucepan of simmering water. Stir until gelatine dissolves. Cool 5 minutes.
4 Beat cheese, sugar and juice in small bowl with electric mixer until smooth; beat in cream. Stir in gelatine mixture.
5 Sprinkle half the raspberries over base; spread with filling. Refrigerate overnight.
6 Blend or process remaining raspberries; strain. Serve cheesecake with berry coulis.

Serves 10

frozen citrus yogurt

500g cream cheese, softened
1 cup (220g) caster sugar
3 cups (800g) vanilla yogurt
1 tablespoon finely grated
  lemon rind
1 tablespoon finely grated
  lime rind
½ cup (120ml) orange juice
⅓ cup (80ml) lemon juice
2 tablespoons lime juice
orange food colouring
⅓ cup (25g) shredded coconut,
  toasted

1 Place a collar of foil around six ¾-cup (180ml) dishes; secure with string.
2 Beat cheese and sugar in medium bowl with electric mixer until smooth. Gradually add yogurt; beat until smooth. Stir in rinds, juices and enough food colouring to tint mixture pale orange.
3 Divide mixture among dishes. Cover loosely with plastic wrap; freeze overnight.
4 Remove cheesecakes from freezer; stand 5 minutes. Remove collars; press coconut around sides of cheesecakes. Freeze 5 minutes before serving.

Serves 6

vanilla slice

2 sheets ready-rolled puff pastry

Custard
½ cup (110g) caster sugar
⅓ cup (50g) cornflour
¼ cup (30g) custard powder
2 cups (500ml) milk
40g butter, chopped
2 egg yolks
2 teaspoons vanilla extract

Filling
1½ teaspoons gelatine
1 tablespoon water
250g cream cheese, softened
⅓ cup (75g) caster sugar
¾ cup (180ml) cream

Passionfruit icing
1½ cups (240g) icing sugar
1 teaspoon soft butter
2 tablespoons passionfruit pulp

1 Preheat oven to 240°C/220°C fan-forced. Grease 23cm square cake pan; line base and sides with foil, extending foil 5cm above edges of pan.
2 Place pastry sheets on greased oven trays; prick all over with a fork. Bake about 10 minutes or until browned well; cool. Flatten pastry sheets; place one sheet into pan.
3 Make custard by blending sugar, cornflour and custard powder in medium saucepan with milk. Stir over heat until mixture boils and thickens. Remove from heat, stir in butter, egg yolks and extract. Pour hot custard over pastry. Cool 15 minutes.
4 Make filling by sprinkling gelatine over the water in small heatproof jug; stand jug in small saucepan of simmering water. Stir until gelatine dissolves. Cool 5 minutes.

5 Beat cheese, sugar and cream in small bowl with electric mixer until smooth. Stir in gelatine mixture; spread over custard in pan, top with remaining pastry, flat side up, press down gently. Refrigerate 4 hours.
6 Make passionfruit icing.
7 Spread pastry with passionfruit icing. Cut slice when icing is set.

Passionfruit icing
Sift icing sugar into small heatproof bowl; stir in butter and passionfruit. Place bowl over saucepan of hot water; stir until icing is spreadable.

Serves 12

useful tips

Cheesecakes are easy to make, and, with the help of these tips, you will have perfect results every time. Baked cheesecakes should be cooled slowly – turn the oven off after they're cooked, then prop the oven door slightly open, using a wooden spoon. Most cheesecakes benefit from being made a day ahead, the flavours develop and the texture becomes firm. Baked cheesecakes are best eaten at room temperature. Use a hot dry sharp knife to cut cheesecakes.

Making a crumb crust that looks good and cuts well depends on fine biscuit crumbs being pressed firmly and evenly into the tin. We use a processor to make fine crumbs, add the butter etc, then pulse to combine ingredients. Press crumbs over the base, then, using a straight-sided glass, press crumbs up the side of the tin.

Beating a cheesecake mixture for a smooth textured result: have the cream cheese, and preferably the other ingredients, at room temperature, before you start to mix. Use the correct sized equipment, and add the ingredients in the order we suggest. Do not over-beat mixtures that contain cream and mascarpone in particular.

Roasting or toasting nuts and coconut is easily done in a frying pan or on an oven tray. Spread the nuts in pan or tray, stir over a medium heat (or, roast in a moderate oven for about 5 minutes) until they're almost as browned as you want them. Spread them out onto a tray to cool.

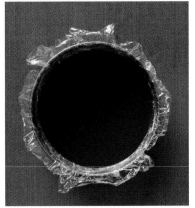

Using a springform tin for cheesecakes eliminates the turning-out process. If you're going to transfer a cheesecake from a springform tin base to a plate, it's a good idea to secure the base upside down in the tin. This will make it easy to push a large spatula or egg slide under the crust, so you can slide the chilled cheesecake onto a plate.

Springform tins are readily available at some supermarkets, kitchenware shops, hardware shops, chain and department stores. Quality and finishes vary too, and you do get what you pay for. If you're serious about making cheesecakes, it's probably smart to buy a good quality tin in a size that suits your needs, and look after it properly.

Lining a springform tin with plastic wrap will give chilled cheesecakes a smooth side. Remove the base of the tin. Drape a long strip of plastic wrap over the lightly greased tin, then position and secure the base back into the tin. This will stretch the wrap neatly, leave a little of the wrap hanging over the edge.

Some fillings, like those containing acidic ingredients such as citrus juice, rhubarb etc, might react slightly where it comes in contact with the tin. Slight discolouration is unattractive, but not harmful to eat. To avoid discolouration, line tins with baking paper for baked cheesecakes, and plastic wrap for chilled cheesecakes.

Tin sizes specified in our recipes match the sizes stamped on the tin's base, not the actual measurement when the tin is closed – be aware of this if you use a regular round cake pan instead. Regular cake pans are also slightly deeper than springform tins, so line the springform tin with a collar of baking paper, extending it about 5cm above the edge of the tin.

Tins with non-stick surfaces do not need to be greased or lined, providing the surface hasn't been damaged.

Always wash and dry tins thoroughly before returning and securing the removable base into the ring part of the tin. This helps you keep track of the base and ensures it stays flat.

glossary

almond
blanched brown skins removed.
flaked paper-thin slices.
meal also known as ground almonds; nuts are powdered to a flour-like texture.
slivered small pieces cut lengthways.

baileys irish cream an irish whiskey and cream-based liqueur.

bicarbonate of soda also known as baking soda.

biscuits
butternut snap crunchy biscuit made from rolled oats, coconut and golden syrup.
chocolate chip plain butter biscuits with chocolate chips.
chocolate cream-filled chocolate biscuits sandwiched together with vanilla cream.
granita also known as digestives; made from wheat flakes.
plain chocolate crunchy biscuit made from cocoa.
plain sweet crisp, sweet and vanilla flavoured.

butter use salted or unsalted ("sweet") butter; 125g is equal to 1 stick of butter. Unsalted butter has no salt added and is perhaps the most popular among pastry-chefs.

cardamom native to India and used extensively in its cuisine; can be purchased in pod, seed or ground form. Has a distinctive aromatic, sweetly rich flavour.

cheese
cream also known as philadelphia or philly; a soft cow-milk cheese with a fat content ranging from 14 to 33 per cent.
cottage fresh, white, unripened curd cheese with a lumpy consistency and mild, sweet flavour. Fat content ranges from 15 to 55 per cent and is determined by whether it is made from whole, low-fat or fat-free cow milk.
light spreadable cream.
low-fat cottage fat content 1 per cent.
low-fat ricotta fat content 9 per cent.
mascarpone an Italian fresh cultured-cream product made in much the same way as yogurt. It is whiteish to creamy yellow in colour, with a buttery-rich, luscious texture.
ricotta a soft, sweet, moist, white cow-milk cheese with a low-fat content (about 11 per cent) and a slightly grainy texture. Its name roughly translates as "cooked again" as its made from a whey that is itself a by-product of other cheese making.

cherry ripe bars dark chocolate bar made with coconut and cherries; standard size bar weighs 55g.

chocolate
dark eating made of cocoa liquor, cocoa butter and sugar.
liqueur we used Cadbury cream liqueur, a chocolate-flavoured liqueur.
milk eating most popular eating chocolate, mild and very sweet; similar in make-up to dark chocolate with the difference being the addition of milk solids.
mud cake a rich, dense, moist cake.

cinnamon stick dried inner bark of the shoots of a cinnamon tree. Used to flavour both sweet and savoury dishes; remove and discard before serving.

cloves dried flower buds of a tropical tree; can be used whole or in ground form. Has a strong scent and taste so should be used minimally.

cocoa powder also called cocoa; unsweetened, dried, roasted then ground cocoa beans.

coconut
desiccated unsweetened, concentrated, dried shredded coconut.
milk not the liquid found inside the fruit (coconut water), but the diluted liquid from the second pressing of the white flesh of a mature coconut (the first pressing produces coconut cream). Available in cans and cartons at most supermarkets.
shredded unsweetened thin strips of dried coconut flesh.

cointreau orange-flavoured liqueur.

corella pears also known as forelle; small to medium in size with a reddish-yellow skin.

cornflour also known as cornstarch.

cranberries tart, red, edible berries. delicious used in jellies, drinks, desserts and sauces.

cream (minimum fat content of 18 per cent) homogenised and pasteurised, also known as single or pouring cream; commonly used in sauces, desserts and soups.
light (minimum fat content of 18 per cent) a light whipping cream containing a thickener.
sour (minimum fat content of 35 per cent) a thick, commercially-cultured soured cream.
thickened (minimum fat content of 35 per cent) a whipping cream containing a thickener.

cream of tartar the acid ingredient in baking powder; added to confectionery mixtures to help prevent sugar crystallising. Keeps frostings creamy and improves volume when beating egg whites.

crème de menthe a sweet, mint-flavoured liqueur.

custard powder instant mixture used to make pouring custard; similar to North American instant pudding mixes.

dark rum we prefer to use an underproof rum (not overproof) for a more subtle flavour.

eggs we use large chicken eggs having an average weight of 60g in our recipes unless stated otherwise. Some recipes in this book call for raw or barely cooked eggs; exercise caution if there is a salmonella problem in your area.

flour
plain an all-purpose flour, made from wheat.
rice a very fine flour, made from ground white rice.
self-raising flour mixed with baking powder in the proportion of 1 cup flour to 2 teaspoons baking powder.

food colouring vegetable-based substance available in liquid, paste or gel form.

frangelico an Italian liqueur flavoured with hazelnuts and spices.

ginger, fresh also known as green or root ginger; the thick gnarled root of a tropical plant. Can be kept, peeled, covered with dry sherry in a jar and refrigerated, or frozen in an airtight container.

gelatine (gelatin) a thickening agent made from either collagen, a protein found in animal connective tissue and bones, or certain algae (agar-agar). We used powdered gelatine as a setting agent. It is also available in sheets called leaf gelatine.

glacé fruit fruit cooked in heavy sugar syrup then dried.

golden delicious apples skin is pale green-yellow in colour with a sweet, crisp flesh.

golden syrup a by-product of refined sugarcane; pure maple syrup or honey can be substituted.

grand marnier a brandy-based orange flavoured liqueur.

hazelnuts also known as filberts; plump, grape-size, rich, sweet nut having a brown inedible skin that is removed by rubbing heated nuts together vigorously in a tea towel.

jam also known as preserve or conserve.

kahlua coffee-flavoured liqueur made in Mexico.

lemon-flavoured spread a commercial lemon curd or lemon butter.

macadamias native to Australia, a rich and buttery nut; store in the refrigerator because of the high oil content.

macaroons a chewy biscuit made with egg white, sugar and coconut or almond meal.

madeira cake similar to a simple pound cake, the top is sprinkled with candied lemon peel halfway through baking; sometimes drizzled with madeira wine.

malibu a coconut-flavoured rum.

maltesers crispy malt balls covered in milk chocolate.

maple syrup distilled from the sap of sugar maple trees found only in Canada and about ten states in the USA. Most often eaten with pancakes or waffles, but also used as an ingredient in baking or in preparing desserts. Maple-flavoured syrup or pancake syrup is not an adequate substitute for the real thing.

marsala a fortified Italian wine produced in the region surrounding the Sicilian city of Marsala; recognisable by its intense amber colour and complex aroma.

milk we used full-cream homogenised milk unless otherwise specified.

buttermilk in spite of its name, it is actually low in fat, varying between 0.6 and 2.0 per cent per 100 ml. The term originally given to the slightly sour liquid left after butter was churned from cream, today it is intentionally made from no-fat or low-fat milk to which specific bacterial cultures have been added during the manufacturing process.

sweetened condensed a canned milk product consisting of milk with more than half the water content removed and sugar added to the milk that remains.

mixed spice a classic mixture generally containing caraway, allspice, coriander, cumin, nutmeg and ginger, although cinnamon and other spices can be added. Used with fruit and in cakes.

nutmeg the dried nut of an evergreen tree native to Indonesia; is available in ground form or you can grate your own with a fine grater.

pecans native to the United States and now grown locally; golden-brown, buttery and rich in flavour.

peppermint crisp chocolate bars crunchy peppermint toffee covered in chocolate.

powdered malt soluble powder made from dried milk, malted barley, and flour.

quince yellow-skinned fruit with hard texture and astringent, tart taste; eaten cooked or as a preserve.

raisins dried sweet grapes.

rind also known as zest; the outer layer of all citrus fruits.

rhubarb a plant with long, green-red stalks; become sweet and edible when cooked.

rosewater extract made from crushed rose petals, called gulab in India; used for its aromatic quality in many desserts.

savoiardi sponge finger biscuits also known as savoy biscuits or ladyfingers; Italian-style crisp biscuits made from a sponge-cake mixture.

semolina coarsely ground flour milled from durum wheat; the flour used in making gnocchi, pasta and couscous.

sponge cake a feather-light, fluffy cake made with sugar, eggs and flour.

sugar we used coarse, granulated table sugar, also known as crystal sugar, unless otherwise specified.
brown a soft, fine granulated sugar containing molasses to give its characteristic colour.
caster also known as superfine or finely granulated table sugar.
demerara small-grained, golden-coloured crystal sugar.
icing also known as confectioners' sugar or powdered sugar; crushed granulated sugar with added cornflour (about 3 per cent).
palm also known as nam tan pip, jaggery, jawa or gula melaka; made from the sap of the sugar palm tree. Light brown to black in colour and usually sold in rock-hard cakes; substitute with brown sugar if hard to find.
white coarse and granulated; also known as table sugar.

vanilla
bean dried long, thin pod from a tropical golden orchid grown in central and South America and Tahiti; the minuscule black seeds inside the bean are used to impart a distinctively sweet vanilla flavour to baking and in desserts.
extract vanilla beans that have been submerged in alcohol. Vanilla essence is not a suitable substitute.

vegetable oil fat extracted from plant sources.

yogurt if a recipe in this book calls for low-fat yogurt, we use one with a fat content of less than 0.2 per cent.

conversion chart

measures

One Australian metric measuring cup holds approximately 250ml; one Australian metric tablespoon holds 20ml; one Australian metric teaspoon holds 5ml.

The difference between one country's measuring cups and another's is within a two- or three-teaspoon variance, and will not affect your cooking results. North America, New Zealand and the United Kingdom use a 15ml tablespoon.

All cup and spoon measurements are level. The most accurate way of measuring dry ingredients is to weigh them. When measuring liquids, use a clear glass or plastic jug with the metric markings.

We use large eggs with an average weight of 60g.

dry measures

METRIC	IMPERIAL
15g	½oz
30g	1oz
60g	2oz
90g	3oz
125g	4oz (¼lb)
155g	5oz
185g	6oz
220g	7oz
250g	8oz (½lb)
280g	9oz
315g	10oz
345g	11oz
375g	12oz (¾lb)
410g	13oz
440g	14oz
470g	15oz
500g	16oz (1lb)
750g	24oz (1½lb)
1kg	32oz (2lb)

liquid measures

METRIC	IMPERIAL
30ml	1 fluid oz
60ml	2 fluid oz
100ml	3 fluid oz
125ml	4 fluid oz
150ml	5 fluid oz (¼ pint/1 gill)
190ml	6 fluid oz
250ml	8 fluid oz
300ml	10 fluid oz (½ pint)
500ml	16 fluid oz
600ml	20 fluid oz (1 pint)
1000ml (1 litre)	1¾ pints

length measures

3mm	⅛in
6mm	¼in
1cm	½in
2cm	¾in
2.5cm	1in
5cm	2in
6cm	2½in
8cm	3in
10cm	4in
13cm	5in
15cm	6in
18cm	7in
20cm	8in
23cm	9in
25cm	10in
28cm	11in
30cm	12in (1ft)

oven temperatures

These oven temperatures are only a guide for conventional ovens. For fan-forced ovens, check the manufacturer's manual.

	°C (CELSIUS)	°F (FAHRENHEIT)	GAS MARK
Very slow	120	250	½
Slow	150	275-300	1-2
Moderately slow	160	325	3
Moderate	180	350-375	4-5
Moderately hot	200	400	6
Hot	220	425-450	7-8
Very hot	240	475	9

index

ARE YOU MISSING SOME OF THE WORLD'S FAVOURITE COOKBOOKS?

The Australian Women's Weekly Cookbooks are available from bookshops, cookshops, supermarkets and other stores all over the world. You can also buy direct from the publisher, using the order form below.

TITLE	RRP	QTY	TITLE	RRP	QTY
Asian, Meals in Minutes	£6.99		Indian Cooking Class	£6.99	
Babies & Toddlers Good Food	£6.99		Japanese Cooking Class	£6.99	
Barbecue Meals In Minutes	£6.99		Kids' Birthday Cakes	£6.99	
Beginners Cooking Class	£6.99		Kids Cooking	£6.99	
Beginners Simple Meals	£6.99		Lean Food	£6.99	
Beginners Thai	£6.99		Low-carb, Low-fat	£6.99	
Best Food	£6.99		Low-fat Feasts	£6.99	
Best Food Desserts	£6.99		Low-fat Food For Life	£6.99	
Best Food Fast	£6.99		Low-fat Meals in Minutes	£6.99	
Best Food Mains	£6.99		Main Course Salads	£6.99	
Cakes Biscuits & Slices	£6.99		Mexican	£6.99	
Cakes Cooking Class	£6.99		Middle Eastern Cooking Class	£6.99	
Caribbean Cooking	£6.99		Midweek Meals in Minutes	£6.99	
Casseroles	£6.99		Muffins, Scones & Breads	£6.99	
Cheesecakes: baked and chilled	£6.99		New Casseroles	£6.99	
Chicken	£6.99		New Classics	£6.99	
Chicken Meals in Minutes	£6.99		New Finger Food	£6.99	
Chinese Cooking Class	£6.99		New Salads	£6.99	
Christmas Cooking	£6.99		Party Food and Drink	£6.99	
Chocolate	£6.99		Pasta Meals in Minutes	£6.99	
Cocktails	£6.99		Potatoes	£6.99	
Cooking for Friends	£6.99		Salads: Simple, Fast & Fresh	£6.99	
Cupcakes & Fairycakes	£6.99		Saucery	£6.99	
Detox	£6.99		Sauces Salsas & Dressings	£6.99	
Dinner Beef	£6.99		Sensational Stir-Fries	£6.99	
Dinner Lamb	£6.99		Short-order Cook	£6.99	
Dinner Seafood	£6.99		Slim	£6.99	
Easy Australian Style	£6.99		Stir-fry	£6.99	
Easy Curry	£6.99		Superfoods for Exam Success	£6.99	
Easy Spanish-Style	£6.99		Sweet Old Fashioned Favourites	£6.99	
Essential Soup	£6.99		Tapas Mezze Antipasto & other bites	£6.99	
French Food, New	£6.99		Thai Cooking Class	£6.99	
Fresh Food for Babies & Toddlers	£6.99		Traditional Italian	£6.99	
Get Real, Make a Meal	£6.99		Vegetarian Meals in Minutes	£6.99	
Good Food Fast	£6.99		Vegie Food	£6.99	
Great Lamb Cookbook	£6.99		Weekend Cook	£6.99	
Greek Cooking Class	£6.99		Wicked Sweet Indulgences	£6.99	
Grills	£6.99		Wok, Meals in Minutes	£6.99	
Healthy Heart Cookbook	£6.99		TOTAL COST:	£	

Mr/Mrs/Ms _____

Address _____

_____ Postcode _____

Day time phone _____ Email* (optional) _____

I enclose my cheque/money order for £ _____

or please charge £ _____

to my: ☐ Access ☐ Mastercard ☐ Visa ☐ Diners Club

PLEASE NOTE: WE DO NOT ACCEPT SWITCH OR ELECTRON CARDS

Card number ☐☐☐☐☐☐☐☐☐☐☐☐☐☐☐☐☐☐

Expiry date _____ 3 digit security code *(found on reverse of card)* _____

Cardholder's name_____ Signature _____

To order: Mail or fax – photocopy or complete the order form above, and send your credit card details or cheque payable to: Australian Consolidated Press (UK), Moulton Park Business Centre, Red House Road, Moulton Park, Northampton NN3 6AQ, phone (+44) (0) 1604 497531 fax (+44) (0) 1604 497533, e-mail books@acpmedia.co.uk or order online at www.acpuk.com
Non-UK residents: We accept the credit cards listed on the coupon, or cheques, drafts or International Money Orders payable in sterling and drawn on a UK bank. Credit card charges are at the exchange rate current at the time of payment.
Postage and packing UK: Add £1.00 per order plus 50p per book.
Postage and packing overseas: Add £2.00 per order plus £1.00 per book.
All pricing current at time of going to press and subject to change/availability.
Offer ends 31.12.2007

* By including your email address, you consent to receipt of any email regarding this magazine, and other emails which inform you of ACP's other publications, products, services and events, and to promote third party goods and services you may be interested in.